Campfire
Treats

Printed in China

Distributed By:

507 Industrial Street
Waverly, IA 50677

ISBN-13: 978-1-56383-434-9
ISBN-10: 1-56383-434-0
Item #2908

Tips for a Relaxing & Fun Campfire

✓ Browse through this book for great ideas.

✓ Gather everything you need (cooking tools, utensils, food, hot pads, tongs) beforehand on a large tray or rimmed baking sheet or in a basket so you can make just one trip to the fire.

✓ Fruit jars, plastic food storage containers and even muffin tins work great for toting ingredients.

✓ Provide a damp cloth or wet wipes for messy fingers.

✓ At the fire, set supplies on a table or blanket so everyone can help themselves.

✓ Sit back, relax and enjoy yourself.

✓ And above all, have fun!

Make it Safe & Enjoyable

✓ Keep your fire contained to a fire pit or build fire on dirt or rocks.

✓ Build fire at least 8' from flammable objects and buildings (getting too close to neighboring tents or houses is always frowned upon by their occupants).

✓ Cooking utensils, food and, of course, the fire itself will be hot, so handle everything with care.

✓ Responsible adult supervision is essential! And remember, as fun as it might sound, it's just never a good idea to chase siblings with a flaming marshmallow or a hot stick!

✓ Only a few people can safely cook around a campfire at once. Take turns and be nice.

✓ Don't forget to extinguish the fire when you're done.

Banana **Boats**

*Mix & match fillings.
The sky's the limit!*

Grab a banana still in the skin, and cut a slit along the inside curve without cutting all the way through. Gently pull apart to make room for filling.

shopping list

- ✓ Bananas
- ✓ Chocolate chips
- ✓ Mini marshmallows
- ✓ Nuts of your choice
- ✓ Any other toppings desired

Then stuff with your favorite goodies and wrap tightly in foil, making sure to keep the filling side up. Place at the edge of the fire or in hot coals.

Cook 8 to 10 minutes until everything's hot and melty. Remove with tongs. Eat with a spoon. **Amazing!**

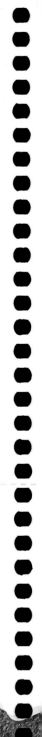

Pizza Pies

Preheat pie iron.

Spray the inside of a hot pie iron with cooking spray. Fit a piece of pizza dough in iron and load with goodies; top with second piece of dough.

shopping list

- ✓ Refrigerated pizza dough
- ✓ Pizza sauce
- ✓ Pepperoni
- ✓ Shredded cheese
- ✓ Any other toppings desired

Close iron, cut off excess dough and hold over coals until bread is toasty brown. Flip and check often so it doesn't burn.

Slide pizza out of iron. Be careful – the filling will be hot! **YUM!**

Fudgy-Orange
Campfire Cakes

These little cakes are great in so many ways! They're perfectly sized for one serving, the orange shell adds yummy flavor, they're cute and – best of all – no dirty plates!

Slice off the top of each orange and hollow out the inside. Set aside the orange flesh to eat along with the finished cake.

shopping list

- ✓ Oranges
- ✓ Your favorite cake or brownie batter
- ✓ Toffee bits, caramel sauce or any other toppings desired

Fill orange shells with batter to within 1″ of the rim to leave room for expansion. Replace the orange top.

Wrap 'em in foil and place in hot coals for 20 to 30 minutes, keeping open end up. Remove with tongs, unwrap and add toppings.

Grab a fork and dig in!

Stuffed
Baby Peppers

shopping list

✓ Baby bell peppers ✓ Feta cheese
✓ Salt & pepper ✓ Green olives

Cut a slit down one side of each pepper; remove seeds (there aren't many). Sprinkle the cavity with salt and pepper. Stuff full of cheese and olives.

Poke a roasting stick through the side of the pepper, making sure it goes nearly through the other side. You don't want to lose this baby in the fire!

Go ahead… that cheese isn't going anywhere. Keep rotating until the pepper is toasted to your liking.

Peppers will blister when done.

Roasted to perfection. **Delish!**

Baked Apple
On a Stick

Push a sharp stick into the bottom of an apple, about halfway through. Hold the apple above hot coals, rotating stick occasionally until the apple skin cracks on all sides.

shopping list

✓ Apples   ✓ Cinnamon/sugar mixture

Carefully remove the skin from the apple with a sharp knife.

Have an adult help.

Now comes the fun part... with the apple still on the stick, roll in the cinnamon/sugar mixture until evenly coated.

13

Campfire
Cones

shopping list

- ✓ Bananas
- ✓ Strawberries
- ✓ Waffle cones
- ✓ Chocolate chips
- ✓ Mini marshmallows
- ✓ Nuts of your choice
- ✓ Any other toppings desired

This is a great snack because there's no mess, and you get to eat the bowl! Chop fruit into small pieces, then set out fillings for mix-and-match fun! Fill the cone nearly full with your choice of goodies, and wrap it all up in foil.

Set on a grate or lay in hot coals for a few minutes until marshmallows are soft and chocolate is gooey. Unwrap and **enjoy!**

Bacon-Cheese *Dogs*

Slice cheese lengthwise into four pieces. Cut a slit in each hot dog, from one end to the other, without cutting through the bottom. Insert one piece of cheese into the slit of each hot dog. Wrap in bacon; secure with toothpicks. Place horizontally on a roasting stick.

shopping list

✓ Hot dogs   ✓ Bacon strips   ✓ String cheese

Hold above fire until bacon is cooked through, rotating stick occasionally (watch out for bacon grease). Patience… Patience…

Try sprinkling with brown sugar before roasting. Yum!

Remove from the stick and chow down! Condiments and buns, optional.

Cheesy Little Smoky Bites

shopping list

- ✓ Little Smokies
- ✓ Cheese curds
- ✓ Refrigerated cresent rolls

Pigs in a Blanket make great finger food, but **THIS**? This is even better because it's cooked over the fire... and there's cheese!

Plunk a sausage and a cheese curd on a crescent roll triangle. Bundle it up tightly so the cheese won't escape.

Brown slowly over hot coals so the dough cooks completely. Rotate the stick for even cooking. You'll be a pro in no time.

Skewer through the smokie to avoid smokie fatality!

Look at all that ooey-gooey cheese! Ohhhh, now that's **GOOD!**

Candy Bar
Sleeves

shopping list

✓ Marshmallows
✓ Mini chocolate
  candy bars

The plain toasted marshmallow goes bold with a chocolate surprise that's just too fun and delicious not to try. Simply place a marshmallow on a sharp stick and push the candy on the end.

Roast carefully so you don't lose the chocolate. When the marshmallow is golden, you know they're done.

Slip the marshmallow over the candy like this.

Mind your fingers. It'll be hot!

Prepare yourself for an amazingly sweet treat!

Cherry
Stick Pies

Spray a 1¼″ dowel with cooking spray. Push a biscuit over end and down sides of dowel, stretching to about 5″ long.

shopping list

- ✓ Refrigerated Grands biscuits
- ✓ Cinnamon/sugar mixture
- ✓ Powdered sugar
- ✓ Pie filling
- ✓ Spray whipped cream

Hold over hot coals until cooked through and toasty brown. Cool for a minute and then twist slightly to remove.

Roast slowly, turning often.

Spray outside of crust with cooking spray; sprinkle with cinnamon/sugar mixture. Sprinkle inside with powdered sugar; then fill with pie filling and whipped cream.

S'mores to Love

While there's nothing wrong with the old standby S'mores made with graham crackers, marshmallows and chocolate bars, why not concoct a more exciting treat? Try this version using a peanut butter cup instead of plain chocolate!

For űber melty-ness, place candy on crackers and set on a metal plate near the fire. Toast marshmallows; then put 'em all together for some outrageous deliciousness!

S'more *fun*

Mix and match to come up with your own combinations.
There's no wrong way to make a S'more!

regular graham crackers with a
regular marshmallow, chocolate
& crisp bacon

cinnamon graham crackers
with a regular marshmallow &
Granny Smith apple slices

chocolate graham crackers
with a strawberry marshmallow,
Nutella & banana slices

regular graham crackers with a
toasted coconut marshmallow,
white chocolate & a fresh
pineapple slice

Breakfast **Hobos**

Preheat pie iron.

Stack buttered bread
(buttered side down),
cheese, sausage, eggs
and buttered bread
(buttered side up) in
pie iron.

shopping list

- ✓ Butter
- ✓ Bread
- ✓ Precooked sausage patties
- ✓ Cheese slices
- ✓ Eggs, beaten

Close. Toast. Eat. Simple, right? It only takes a couple minutes on each side.

No fast food chain required for this breakfast sandwich! **Simply scrumptious!**

Fireside
French Toast

Sprinkled with powdered sugar and dipped in syrup, it's a fun way to make... **breakfast on a stick!**

Mix together eggs, milk and cinnamon/sugar mixture the way you normally make French toast. Cut bread and fruit into bite-size pieces. Dip bread into egg mixture.

shopping list

- ✓ Eggs
- ✓ Milk
- ✓ Cinnamon/sugar mixture
- ✓ French Bread
- ✓ Fruit of choice
- ✓ Powdered sugar
- ✓ Maple syrup

Thread onto a skewer along with your favorite fruit.

Roast slowly until bread is toasted. Just keep on rotating.

Sandwich
Skewers

shopping list

- ✓ French bread
- ✓ Mayonnaise
- ✓ Ham slices
- ✓ Swiss cheese slices
- ✓ Pickle slices
- ✓ Butter

Slice bread and cut slices in half. Spread with mayo, and add ham, cheese and pickles like any sandwich. Butter outside of slices; slide sandwich onto a roasting stick, making sure to skewer those pickles, too!

Hold over hot coals until bread is toasted and cheese is a bit melted. Remove from the stick and **enjoy!**

Quick
Quesadillas

A quick and easy way to enjoy quesadillas…fireside. First, finely chop mushrooms, green onions and red peppers. Then cover half of a tortilla with cheese and veggies. Fold uncovered half over filling.

shopping list

- ✓ Fresh mushrooms
- ✓ Green onions
- ✓ Red peppers
- ✓ Flour tortillas
- ✓ Shredded cheese
- ✓ Any other toppings desired

Wrap in heavy-duty foil, double folding edges to seal.
Lay pack directly on hot coals for 5 to 10 minutes or until cheese melts; remove with tongs.

Try with just cheese, too!

Let cool slightly, then open pack. Cut into smaller pieces or just eat the whole thing. Yeah, it's that good!

Camper **Donuts**

Kitchen shears work great!

Cut each biscuit into quarters. Round the edges. Thread onto a sharp stick, leaving space between each.

shopping list

- ✓ Refrigerated Grands biscuits
- ✓ Melted butter
- ✓ Cinnamon/sugar mixture

Hold over hot coals, roasting slowly so the biscuits cook through. You don't want uncooked donuts!

Roll toasted biscuits in butter and then in cinnamon/sugar mixture. **M-M-M!**

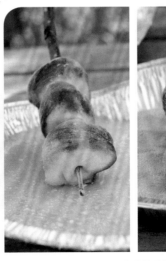

shopping list

- ✓ Frozen French fries
- ✓ Chili, any variety
- ✓ Shredded Cheddar cheese
- ✓ Cooked bacon
- ✓ Green onions

Chili Cheese Fries

This is so easy and delicious, you'll wonder why you never tried it before! First, spray a large piece of heavy-duty foil with cooking spray. Then, dump a bag of frozen French fries in a single layer in the center.

Spread chili over the top and sprinkle with cheese. Chop bacon and green onions and scatter over cheese.

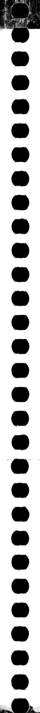

Seal foil tightly around fries and set directly in hot coals for 20 to 25 minutes or until the cheese is melted and the fries are soft.

Carefully open packet and let the hungry mob help themselves to a hot and cheesy chili treat.

Philly
Cheesesteaks

Spray the inside of a hot pie iron with cooking spray. Cut dough to fit in iron. Sandwich beef, cheese, onion and pepper between two dough pieces.

shopping list

- ✓ Refrigerated French bread dough
- ✓ Deli roast beef
- ✓ Cheese slices
- ✓ Onion, sliced
- ✓ Bell pepper, sliced

Close the iron and put in the coals until bread is roasty-toasty brown. Check often so it doesn't burn.

That cheese is a sight to behold, and it tastes even better than it looks!

Mini Lemon
Pies

This campfire treat is sweet and tangy, warm and toasty. And best of all, you can pick it up and eat it with your hands.

Just three simple ingredients and you have a treat that ranks high on the deliciousness scale!

✓ Shortcakes   ✓ Lemon curd   ✓ Mini marshmallows

Set a grate high above warm coals. Set shortcakes on grate, hollow side down, until toasted. (Watch them closely.)

Flip shortcakes over and immediately fill with lemon curd and marshmallows. Let set until the bottoms get toasty and mallows get a bit soft. **Yum!**

41

Taco Bowl
Treats

Flatten a biscuit with your fingers. Wrap heavy-duty foil around the end of a dowel to make a bowl shape about 2½″ in diameter; secure to dowel with more foil.

shopping list

✓ Refrigerated Grands biscuits   ✓ Cooked taco meat   ✓ Your favorite taco fillings

Spray the foil bowl with cooking spray. Set a biscuit on top, stretching it about 2″ down the side.

Hold above hot coals until cooked through, turning often so the dough browns evenly. Cool slightly before removing.

Fill with your favorite taco ingredients.

Brie
Bread

shopping list

- ✓ Round Ciabatta loaf
- ✓ Strawberry jam
- ✓ Brie cheese round
- ✓ Maple syrup
- ✓ Brown sugar

Remove top of loaf and hollow out bread. Add some jam, the cheese, more jam and a little syrup and brown sugar.

Replace top of bread before wrapping loaf in heavy-duty foil. Set in a foil pan on a grate over hot coals for 20 minutes or until hot and gooey. Slice bread and serve warm. **So tasty!**

Pineapple
Upside-Down Cakes

This sweet and simple dessert is a toss-together treat that tastes like it's fresh from the oven.

To prepare, cut pineapple and pound cake into 1″ pieces. Spray a double layer of foil with cooking spray.

shopping list

- ✓ Pineapple
- ✓ Pound cake
- ✓ Maraschino cherries
- ✓ Brown sugar
- ✓ Butter

Pile pineapple, pound cake and cherries in the middle of the foil. Sprinkle with a little brown sugar, and add a few pats of butter.

Fold the foil over the top and seal the ends nice and tight. Set the packets in hot coals for 5 to 10 minutes. Open carefully. Feast your eyes and delight your taste buds!

Popcorn
Packs

Oil & popcorn on 18" piece of heavy-duty foil

Fold foil in half; double-fold those edges. Fold up sides to seal in kernels and oil. Leave some space in there for that wild popping corn.

shopping list

✓ 2 T. popcorn kernels   ✓ 2 T. canola oil   ✓ Salt to taste

Poke a sharp stick through the double folds and hold pouch over flames, shaking often. Continue shaking until popping slows. Let pack cool a bit before opening.

Sprinkle with salt & enjoy!

Now, you can share that bag of corn. Or not.

shopping list

- ✓ Sourdough loaf
- ✓ Mozzarella cheese
- ✓ Mushrooms
- ✓ Melted butter
- ✓ Garlic powder
- ✓ Italian seasoning

Stuffed Cheese Bread

Slice the bread lengthwise and crosswise without cutting through the bottom. Set the loaf in the center of a large double layer of foil sprayed with cooking spray.

Slice cheese and mushrooms and load into cuts. Drizzle butter into the cuts and sprinkle with garlic powder and Italian seasoning.

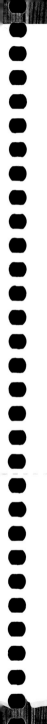

Seal foil around loaf; set packet in a foil baking pan and place the whole thing on a grate over hot coals. Cook for 20 to 25 minutes or until cheese is melted. Rotate bread halfway through cooking time. Open packet and prepare yourself for total awesomeness!

Ooooo melty cheese!

Fire-Roasted
Pickle Wraps

* Toothpicks can help secure bacon.

Push one end of bacon on a sharp stick. Add pickle and wrap with bacon, attaching other end to tip of stick.*

shopping list

✓ Bacon strips   ✓ Whole dill pickles   ✓ Cream cheese, softened

Roast slowly
over the fire until
bacon is done and
pickle blisters.

*Cream cheese
makes these
incredible!*

Strawberry
Shortcakes

Spray the inside of a preheated pie iron with cooking spray. Stack one cake slice, strawberries, chips and a second cake slice in iron, thick sides of cake on opposite ends.

shopping list

✓ Angel food cake, sliced about 1" thick

✓ Strawberries, sliced

✓ White chocolate chips

Close the iron and hold over hot coals for a few minutes, rotating iron. These cook fast, so check often.

Remove from iron and take a nice big bite. **S-o-o-o good!**

Big Dogs-
Campfire Style

Nothing says campfire food like hot dogs! When you can make a dog and bun in one, it's big dog heaven!

Wrap the breadstick strips around the hot dogs, mummy-style.

shopping list

✓ Hot dogs   ✓ Refrigerated breadstick dough

Skewer and roast
ever-so-slowly
over hot coals until
nicely browned.

*Keep rotating
for even cooking.*

Tah-Dah! Now all
you have to do
is devour these
delicious big dogs!
Dip 'em in ketchup
and mustard, if
you like, or eat 'em
plain. Either way,
it's all good!

Strawberry
Meringues

shopping list

✓ Strawberries ✓ Melted chocolate ✓ Marshmallow Fluff
candy wafers

Dip delicious ripe strawberries in melted chocolate (you can melt it right at the fire).

Let chocolate harden, then dip in fluff.

Thread a berry onto a skewer and hold over hot coals to toast. Take care not to place directly in flames. Fluff will turn golden when done.

Toasted Coconut Pumpkin Pies

If you like pumpkin pie, you've gotta try this! Butter bread slices; add one to hot pie iron, buttered side down. Add pie filling and a few marshmallows. Top with a bread slice, buttered side up.

shopping list

- ✓ Butter
- ✓ Bread
- ✓ Pumpkin pie filling
- ✓ Coconut marshmallows

Close the iron and cut off excess bread before holding in hot coals. Keep it in there for a couple of minutes on each side until the bread is nicely toasted, checking often.

These taste best piping hot, but don't burn yourself when you take that first big bite.

Foiled
Peaches

shopping list

- ✓ Butter
- ✓ Brown sugar
- ✓ Fresh peaches, halved, pitted
- ✓ Orange juice

Cut 1 tablespoon butter into small pieces and toss in the center of a large piece of heavy-duty foil. Sprinkle with some brown sugar. Set peach halves on the brown sugar, cut side up.

Top each peach half with more butter and brown sugar. Add about 2 tablespoons orange juice.

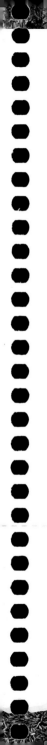

Fold up the foil, sealing all edges, and set on a grate above hot coals for 10 to 15 minutes.

Rotate pack halfway through cooking time.

Carefully take a peak inside. If the peaches are soft and surrounded by a buttery glaze, they're done to perfection.

What's Inside